Unleashing the Power of Data with Trusted AI

A guide for board members and executives

Wendy Turner-Williams

packt

BIRMINGHAM—MUMBAI

Unleashing the Power of Data with Trusted AI

Publisher: Vishal Bodwani
Product Manager: Sathya Mohan
Development Editor: Afzal Shaikh
Lead Development Editors: Siddhant Jain and Oorja Mishra
Copy Editor: Safis Editing
Proofreader: Safis Editing
Project Coordinator: Yash Basil
Production Designer: Deepak Chavan
First published: April 2024
Production reference: 1010724

Published by Packt Publishing Ltd.
Livery Place, 35 Livery Street, Birmingham, B3 2PB, UK.
ISBN 978-1-83546-789-3

www.packt.com

Executive summary

Enter the realm where data becomes the catalyst for innovation and generative AI emerges as the beacon guiding executives and board members through the dynamic landscape of business transformation. Dive into this comprehensive guide, illuminating the synergy between data and AI and how you can fast-track your journey with the use of generative AI. This report is designed to elevate your strategic vision and redefine your organization's success.

This definitive handbook covers the following topics:

- **Generative AI demystified**: Embark on the AI journey with a walkthrough of the evolution and applications of AI. Uncover its power to revolutionize industries, elevate decision-making, and forge the path to unparalleled innovation.
- **Data mastery and AI fusion**: Explore the harmonious integration of data and AI, unraveling the strategies to use these pillars for business transformation. Discover how this synergy accelerates decision-making and creates sustainable competitive advantages.
- **Real-life transformations**: Engage with captivating case studies spotlighting industry giants such as Starbucks, UPS, Netflix, and Siemens. Witness how the fusion of data and AI catalyzed their success stories, reshaping markets and redefining customer experiences.

- **Ethical AI in action**: Navigate the ethical intricacies of AI implementation with precision. Learn how to instill ethical considerations into the DNA of your AI endeavors, fostering trust and responsibility at every turn.

- **Data by Design framework**: Discover the critical pillar of *Data by Design*—a strategic approach embedding data intent, quality, ethical considerations, privacy, and security into the fabric of your data operations. Unveil its power to fortify your organization's data practices, aligning them seamlessly with strategic business goals.

Unleashing the Power of Data with Trusted AI is more than a guide; it is your indispensable roadmap to navigating the realm where data unleashes its full potential. Tailored explicitly for board members, executives, innovators, and tech enthusiasts, this immersive guide promises to reshape your perception of data and AI and their transformative synergy.

Empower your organization to embrace a future where data and generative AI blend seamlessly, leading to innovation, growth, and sustained success.

Target audience

This report targets executives and board members of mid to large enterprises as well as AI, data, ethics, privacy, and security professionals.

Contents

Introduction to AI and generative AI

In today's fast-paced digital landscape, the quest for high-value data insights has become the cornerstone of organizational success. It is a critical market differentiator in a real-time, device-connected modern society. The convergence of data and advanced technologies has unleashed a powerful tool: artificial intelligence (AI). At the nexus of innovation, generative AI, a specific form of AI, stands poised to revolutionize how businesses harness data to engage customers, transform decision-making, and drive operational efficiencies.

Generative AI represents a paradigm shift in technology, empowering machines not only to comprehend and process data but also to create and generate new content, imitating human-like cognitive functions. The underlying premise of generative AI lies in its ability to learn from vast datasets, understand patterns, and subsequently generate content, whether it is natural language, images, graphs, or other forms of data. AI can be looked at as a new type of advanced analytics or decision-making tool that applies your data to content, engagements, and processes. The recent advances in these areas have unleashed generative AI in all aspects of life.

Three types of AI

Artificial narrow intelligence (ANI)

Machine learning
Focuses on specific domains to solve targeted problems

Artificial general intelligence (AGI)

Machine intelligence
Denotes computers with human-level intelligence across various domains

Artificial super intelligence (ASI)

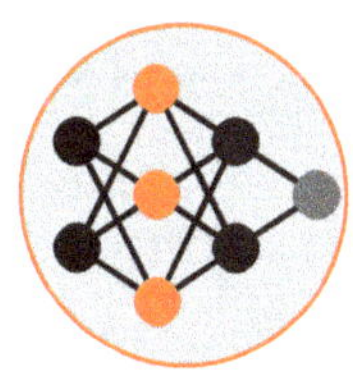

Machine consciousness
Represents intellect surpassing even the most capable human minds in virtually every field

A journey through the AI evolution

The landscape of AI has traversed a remarkable evolutionary path, transforming from theoretical concepts to tangible solutions. Initially conceived as an ambitious pursuit to replicate human intelligence in machines, AI has evolved exponentially, navigating through several phases of development. To grasp the full potential of generative AI, it is important to explore some of the pivotal events and visionaries who have set the AI stage.

1950 – 1970:

- **Inception**: Alan Turing and John McCarthy laid the groundwork for AI.
- **Early stages**: Emergence of symbolic reasoning and logic-based problem solving.

1980 – 1990:

- **Challenges**: AI faced setbacks like the machine translation failure.
- **AI winter**: Lack of funding and progress led to setbacks.
- **Progress**: Expert systems with rule-based AI emerged.

2000 – 2010:

- **Surge of big data AI**: Cloud computing and machine learning fueled AI.
- **Breakthroughs**: Deep learning powered significant advancements.

- **Data revolution**: Data-driven cultures emerged globally.

Early 2010:

- **Generative AI**: Generative adversarial networks (GANs) revolutionized generative AI.
- **Synthetic data**: GANs enabled generation of synthetic data.

Mid to late 2010:

- **IoT impact**: IoT led to a surge in data.
- **Democratization of data**: Access to diverse data fueled innovation.
- **Advancements**: AI made leaps in image synthesis, natural language processing, text generation, and music composition.
- **Ethical concerns**: Challenges with data management and ethical AI outcomes.

It's this rich tapestry of people and technology woven over decades that has now set the stage for everyday AI, powering the world into the AI era.

Unveiling the power of generative AI

Generative AI, at its core, represents a monumental shift in the modern market. Today's consumer has an insatiable appetite for personalized, data-driven experiences in real time. In fact, it is predicted that AI will inject over $15.7 trillion[1] to the global economy by 2030, highlighting its substantial market opportunity.

$15.7 trillion

AI's potential economic impact by 2030

AI applications span industries transforming content creation in marketing to personalizing entertainment recommendations, revolutionizing healthcare diagnostics[2] and personalized medicine, streamlining manufacturing processes through virtual prototyping, and enhancing customer service interactions via digital empathy and advanced chatbots. This seismic shift in AI will redefine human interactions with technology, learning, and even social connections. As AI takes on routine tasks, it will herald a renaissance of human creativity and collective empathy, providing newfound freedom for artistic, intellectual, and social exploration.

While this burgeoning technology is poised to revolutionize industries, everyday AI also introduces unprecedented challenges. The complexities of missing, unclear, and disparate regulatory hurdles, copyright[3] challenges, data poisoning, and ethical concerns such as algorithmic bias are significant legal risks.

In fact, in the United States, numerous laws and regulations, such as the FTC Act, the Fair Credit Reporting Act, and the Equal Credit Opportunity Act (ECOA), ensure protections from algorithmic bias. There's also a notable threat of class-action lawsuits, as evidenced by the case with United Health Group (UHG).[4]

Likewise, in the European Union (EU), the risks are similarly substantial, even prior to the implementation of the AI Act. The General Data Protection Regulation (GDPR) specifically addresses algorithmic decision-making in Article 22(1) and (4), establishing distinct rights and legal frameworks that companies must adhere to.

The lack of focus on data management means organizations must now grapple with years of data debt, as the center stage risk is the data itself. To mitigate this risk, organizations must focus on data management maturity and embrace a Data by Design approach to meet bias, compliance, ethics, and quality concerns.

Navigating the AI transformation is now an essential board mandate. The rising market opportunity demands proactive leadership that steers AI effectively, balancing business benefits with the risk of unethical or even harmful AI impact on your customers, your brand, and society. Leaders must embrace this transformative power, utilizing it as a catalyst for agility, creativity, innovation, and operational efficiency within their organizations.

Modernizing the boardroom to steer data and AI

The expertise provided and methods proposed by boards of directors of the past are outdated and inadequate for today's standards of quality, ethics, and responsible use practices. Leadership roles for boards and executives must evolve significantly, extending well beyond merely maximizing profits or maintaining organizational stability. The emergence of everyday AI has broadened responsibilities, introducing ethical dilemmas, bias mitigation, and a much deeper understanding of data management intricacies and execution.

> "
> **46% of boardroom learders stated that generative AI is currently their main priority above anything else."**

This seismic shift extends beyond mere technological adaptation; it permeates every facet of an organization with the board of directors playing a pivotal role in orchestrating this transformative journey. As organizations grapple with the colossal task of integrating AI, a boardroom metamorphosis is inevitable. Embracing this change requires a deep introspection of the status quo; an understanding that AI adoption demands a deeper insight into data and its responsible use along with the acknowledgement that to do so, change will touch every corner of the organizational framework. This change reaches the highest echelons of leadership—the board of directors and executive leadership. This realization is reflected in 46% of boardroom leaders stating that generative AI is currently their "main priority above anything else."[5]

One might ask, why is AI a board concern? Well, the introduction of AI technologies means the board's fiduciary responsibility extends far beyond corporate profit. Boards are responsible for the health of the company and the management of company risk. This includes bridging various stakeholder interests, including customers, employees, shareholders, communities, and now society at large. The board's oversight is crucial in ensuring that AI initiatives prioritize ethical considerations, maintain quality standards, protect privacy, address new security challenges, and adhere to regulatory compliance, thereby upholding stakeholders' trust and confidence in the organization.

91.9%

Executives cite cultural barriers as the principal obstacle

8.1%

Executives cite technology limitations as the primary impediment

The complex nature of AI technologies demands a strategic and structured approach. AI is fueled by one thing and one thing only—your data. Therefore, systemic cultural changes are required to overcome the challenges of scaling data and analytics. Over 90% of executives—91.9% in 2022—point to culture as the greatest impediment to achieving this business outcome. Only 8.1% cite technology limitations as the primary impediment.[6]

The appointment of a Chief Data and AI Officer (CDAIO) will be of paramount importance in this new paradigm. Reporting directly to the CEO and the board, this figure should be responsible for crafting comprehensive data and AI strategies and implementing tactical approaches, while weighing and devising risk mitigation measures for the organization's AI initiatives. Their role is central to ensuring that AI integration aligns with the organization's data offense and defense objectives.

The offense and defense of data

When it comes to corporate organizations, you have functions that often play an offensive or defensive role within the business. If you think about physical data as an American football, the role of a CDAIO is to ensure the ball is effectively managed and moved to meet your strategic objective—in football's case, a touchdown. The players on your offensive team represent your offense business functions (sales, customer success, marketing, product, etc.). There is also a defensive aspect to data; you don't want your competitors or the bad guys to get your data, and you definitely do not want them to score with it.

With this concept in mind, you can think about data strategies often having offense and defense aspects.

An offensive strategy may be to determine how to enable go-to-market (GTM) insights to ensure new customers, industries, or geo sales. Or how do you set up event triggers that collect customer journey details to improve user experience, or to even upsell another product? Or how do you integrate mergers and acquisitions (M&A) data to enable new opportunities or new platform services to improve agility and speed to insights?

A defensive strategy might be the creation of a data categorization standard to ensure all data is tagged with a common taxonomy to enable new operational improvements related to right-to-be-forgotten lineage tracking or to improve impact assessment capabilities related to a breach. Data policy publication is important so people understand what is expected and who is accountable. Many Data by Design principles related to data handling are a mix of offense and defense, such as data modeling to ensure data linkability for new insights, aggregating data to reduce the risk of personal data being leaked, or the use of anonymization to mask personal data.

Data is an art of offense and defense. It's also a team sport where every organization wants to move or protect the ball for the team.

Navigating the future of AI by bridging strategies

As organizations embark on the groundbreaking AI revolution, it becomes increasingly evident that while AI stands as a monumental technological advancement, its cornerstone lies in the realm of data. It has been estimated that 75%[7] of organizations are expected to establish a centralized data and analytics data center of excellence by 2024, which necessitates stringent checks, robust health standards, and rigorous safety protocols to ensure accountability, maintain data quality, and regulate usage effectively.

75%

of organizations will have a centralized data and analytics data center of excellence by 2024

The adage *garbage in, garbage out* rings especially true in the context of generative AI. The quality of data consumed and then produced directly influences its behavior and outcomes. AI can be seen as a unique data consumer and producer, wielding extraordinary capabilities.

While water cooler discussions on the future of AI often evoke concerns about artificial general intelligence (AGI) or singularity—or worse, dystopian scenarios—the true concern should center on overseeing the data that AI interacts with, ensuring ethical decision-making and managing the social impact of its outputs. The challenge lies in fostering an empathetic environment that forges strategic connections while embracing a Data by Design approach to cultivate a culture steeped in ethics, business understanding, data literacy, and critical-thinking skills.

What is Data by Design?

Data by Design refers to an approach in data engineering that extends the traditional design phase to not only ensure the technical architecture of data systems but also focus on various aspects related to data quality, management maturity, intended use, and risk prevention. It encompasses a comprehensive strategy to deliberately shape and structure data systems while considering potential risks such as privacy concerns, geo-residency, access control, biases, and ethical implications. In essence, it is an inclusive framework that emphasizes the proactive consideration and integration of risk management strategies throughout the entire life cycle of data, from its initial conception to its utilization in different applications.

Data by Design involves the following:

- **Data architecture and platforms**: These are key to naming, taxonomy, data linkability, reusable design frameworks, scalability, performance, velocity, and self-service capabilities.
- **Data quality assurance**: Ensuring the accuracy, completeness, consistency, and reliability of data throughout its life cycle.

- **Data management maturity**: Implementing processes, policies, and best practices to efficiently handle, store, and utilize data, aligned with industry standards.
- **Intended use of data**: Clearly defining and understanding the purpose and application of data to ensure it aligns with business objectives and ethical considerations.
- **Risk prevention**: Identifying and mitigating potential risks associated with data, including privacy concerns, geographical restrictions, access control issues, biases in algorithms or data, and ethical implications.
- **Compliance and ethics**: Ensuring that data handling and utilization comply with legal regulations, industry standards, and ethical guidelines.

Data engineers, data analysts, data scientists, and machine learning experts should be trained to incorporate Data by Design as an integral part of their workflow. By integrating these principles into their workflows, professionals involved in handling data can create systems that are not only technically robust but also ethical, compliant, and capable of minimizing risks associated with data misuse, privacy breaches, biases, and other potential issues.

The strategic ring that binds us

Frequently, companies hurriedly adopt new technology, enticed by its novelty, but devoid of a comprehensive grasp of strategic business objectives or the data required to achieve those objectives. This technological *magic bullet* approach often yields suboptimal ROI, creating business silos and escalating risks due to a lack of a cohesive, long-term strategy that interlaces business goals with data and infrastructure planning.

Going forward, business, data, and infrastructure initiatives must be vetted against three pillars: *people*, *process*, and *technology*.

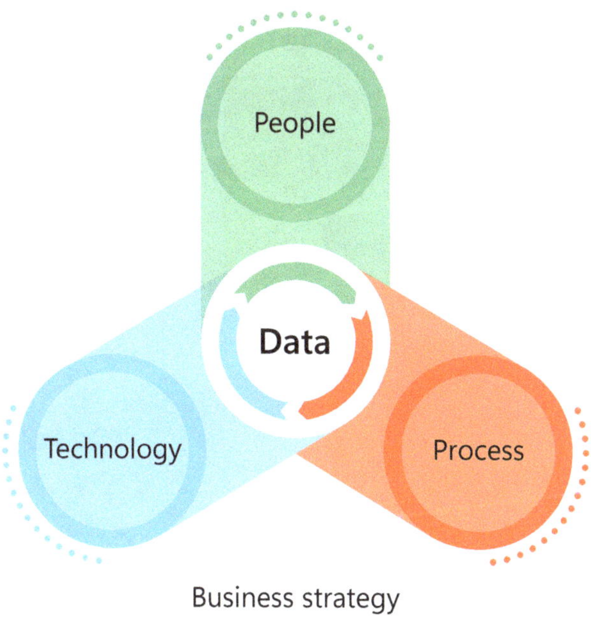

Board members and executives must embrace this holistic strategic imperative to sow the seeds of an ethical, quality, and trusted AI journey. To do this, organizations must understand that business, data, and infrastructure strategies are parts of a holistic system, analogous to the human body, where each strategy plays a pivotal role:

- **Business strategy**: Guides and coordinates organizational activities, responds to changes, communicates, decides, adapts, and rallies the team.

- **Data strategy**: Ingests, creates, and eliminates data to fuel processes, decisions, monitoring, and outcomes. Transforms data into actionable intelligent insights that fuel the activities, responses, decisions, and communications across the organization.

- **Infrastructure strategy**: Provides the structural support, protection, and facilitation of business process movement, allowing the organization to act and adapt in the market.

AI serves as an intricate extension of these processes, a highly sophisticated mechanism that consumes data to perform tasks or make decisions. Rather than considering a separate AI strategy, it is more effective to perceive AI as an integral part of the existing data strategy since, fundamentally, AI is similar to an advanced analytics layer, it's another consumer and producer of data.

In this light, the crux of AI risks and opportunities lies within your data. The challenge is ensuring the data AI interacts with is quality, robust, relevant, and dependable while also meeting compliance, ethics, and regulatory requirements.

“

Rather than considering a separate AI strategy, it is more effective to perceive AI as an integral part of the existing data strategy.”

Seven steps to ethical, quality, and trusted generative AI implementation

Having emphasized the critical role of business, data, and infrastructure strategies, alongside the concept of Data by Design, it is time to take tactical strides in your AI journey. Assessing organizational readiness is a foundational aspect of defining the explicit steps of your journey and the unique detours needed along the way. As only 35%[8] of companies consider themselves adequately prepared for AI implementation, you should think of these steps as your AI trip advisor. The AI trip advisor defines the *who*, *what*, *what if*, *when*, *why*, and *where* of your journey.

35%

of companies consider themselves adequately prepared for AI implementation.

Every industry and company has its own unique strategy, organizational structure, people, infrastructure, data, engineering processes, and risks. This report is written to help boards of directors and executives with their generative AI journey—it's your AI trip advisor companion. The recommendations may seem like a top-down approach as a result, but if you read between the lines, the report focuses on understanding the criticality of data to AI, the need to understand AI risks, a starting point for generative AI implementation, and the introduction of the Data by Design concept, which not only balances business needs but also ensures that the data itself is consumed, stored, handled, and shared at inception with quality, bias, ethics, and legal or regulatory data-handling requirements in mind. This pairs the on-ground experts with the executives, as knowledge sharing is required in order for a board member or executive to have visibility and insight. This guide can be used to help uplevel details to your executive layer.

A personal journey in Azure engineering

I would like to provide a personal example of a Data by Design initiative that had a top-down, bottom-up, and side-to-side approach all at once. Years ago, when Azure was in its initial stages, I was responsible for the Azure Data Platform's Engineering Fundamentals program. This program was the result of strategy and technology shifts, as Azure was in its infancy and many of the employees had originally worked in a box product environment. The concept of shipping in a day was foreign, as was building products on top of other infrastructure cloud services that were also shipping in a day. We needed to shift engineering fundamentals left to ensure available, extensible, supportable, and trusted services.

To do this, we had to significantly invest in frameworks, training, process automation, and monitoring to assess the maturity of each product against standardized architecture, engineering, support, and risk management processes. This included fundamentals like business continuity and disaster recovery (BCDR), capacity planning, compliance, fault modeling, incident management, privacy, security, and worldwide readiness—along with many others. This was a total culture change, and it was not always popular with the engineers. It also required significant top-down effort by the executives to continuously reinforce the needed behaviors, design patterns, due diligence, and steps. The goal was not to require top-down direction, or decisioning; the goal was to embed critical thinking, processes, tools, and risk awareness into the architects, engineers, product managers themselves to improve long-term agility, availability, elasticity, innovation, and trust—the goal was a trusted service by design.

It did not take long before the training sessions naturally began to drive impact and design changes within the engineering teams. Engineering leads found value with the fault-modeling process to identify risky dependencies or how a pen test helped them get through security approvals. This resulted in reduced incidents and improved designs that reduced compliance, security, or fault risks while lowering risks.

Data by Design is no different, in fact it is just one area of focus versus the 20 we needed to shift to cover Azure Engineering Fundamentals as a whole. Designing for quality, ethical, trusted AI can be intuitive, and just a normal aspect of a requirement, design, code, and trust review—it should be a core component of your SDLC process.

Step 1: People and processes – executive R&R model and AI task force

The mainstay of a successful AI transformation lies in a robust, clear executive roles and responsibilities model. As organizations differ in structure, aligning to a guideline that guarantees essential expertise and accountability is critical.

Just as a football team uses offense, defense, special teams, and so on to work harmoniously, organizations operate through interconnected departments and processes. Data, akin to a company's lifeblood, courses through these systems, profoundly influencing the overall vitality and efficiency. Yet, like any complex organism, internal politics often affect the health and productivity of these data systems. Steering a data and AI strategy demands a single accountable P&L executive whose sole charge is to treat data and AI as a core enterprise asset and to manage its risks. This leader ensures data alignment with strategic business needs, promotes responsible and quality data usage, navigates through internal politics, and wields the authority required for effective data management.

If one part of the system falters, the entire organization might falter. You will often find that data is the root cause of many of your organizational ailments. This is usually due to the lack of a clear data strategy and management, such as a dedicated Chief Data and AI Officer (CDAIO).

"Data is the root cause of many of your organizational ailments."

Without this pivotal role or with misaligned responsibilities under other functions, inefficiency and conflict ensue, akin to an orchestra without a conductor.[9]

Orchestrating the symphony of AI

Continuing with the conductor analogy, imagine data as the notes, tempo, and pauses in music. Each department is represented by an instrument type, and the data strategy is to ensure that each musician and section performs to their finest. When the raw notes on paper are infused with the individual musician's skill, and the various instrument types intertwine and work in unison to build a score—even the silence between the beats are part of the story, the emotion.

When we think of AI, the musicians are more like wind-up toy versions of ourselves—who only act and react based on the data they have been programed with. This wind-up toy version doesn't have common sense, it doesn't understand your company strategy, operations, or tribal knowledge. It can play the instrument, but it doesn't understand the beat or the song the rest of your team is playing. You must ensure your wind-up musicians are fed the best nutrients, the best data, and you must watch how the musicians react, behave, and make proper adjustment before putting the musician into a live audience show.

Ensuring comprehensive data and AI oversight with stewards

To ensure a healthy, positively impactful AI journey, teams such as compliance, ethics, privacy, risk, and security must function as internal regulators, ensuring integrity and security. While these functions often work in silos, as discipline subject matter experts (SMEs), when it comes to a quality, ethical, and trusted AI future, bridging these silos is incredibly important.

The very concept of data as an asset implies a value and a risk. When you think of compliance, data, ethics, privacy, risk, and security teams, they are sister disciplines that specialize in performing their function. In organizations, this often results in organizational silos right down the offense and defense line. When it comes to data, these silos can be detrimental. A data team that does not consume with intent or properly apply access control or rule-based data-handling principles such as anonymization or geo-residency principles amplifies the compliance, regulatory, and compliance risks. The reverse can be said of a privacy, risk, or cybersecurity teams that overly focuses on defense without understanding the organization's offensive data needs and the ways that data management, trusted data platform services, or mature data engineering can mitigate data risks from the very beginning. Offense and defense must be weighed, and now, with data-fed AI, you must also weigh things such as quality, bias, and ethics. You need a holistic, repeatable approach with the right weights to ensure balance.

Example: Balanced approach

Here is an example illustrating the delicate balance achieved of offense and defense in my own capacity as a CDAIO. In a previous role, I spearheaded the modernization of our data strategy, data management processes, data platforms and services while concurrently enhancing the quality, reliability, and trust of the data housed within these platforms and mitigating data risks.

One notable project involved the migration of product logs and instrumentation from an expensive and limited on-premises Hadoop instance to a more flexible, scalable, and innovative cloud-based infrastructure. Rather than a simple lift-and-shift approach, we divided the initiative into three parallel tracks:

- **People and processes**: Understanding existing consumers/producers and their data use cases to identify opportunities to improve the data itself. This touched every organization in the company and included use cases like product debugging, customer security incident response team (CSIRT) customer response, product search, analytics, data science and machine learning models.

- **Data**: Drove data management maturity to improve stewardship, policy reinforcement, quality, data lifecycle gaps, and data risk management to clean data prior to migration, and to ensure known policy and correct data management automation in the new environment.

- **Technology**: The technical architecture, use cases, and features along with the engineering deliverables are required to stabilize the current state, migrate data to the new environment, and integrate the new environment, services, and features with our other data platform services.

Through this multi-lens approach, we accomplished several key objectives:

- Self-funded two years of infrastructure by establishing clear and universally agreed-upon policies for retaining raw logs and enforcing these policies effectively.
- Reduced the time to migrate and data swamps by cleaning data pre-migration.
- Developed an optimized, regulated, and high-performance standard schema for logs that satisfied 95% of cross-functional analytics requirements. This resulted in substantial reductions in data processing costs, duplication, overall risk, and a marked improvement in data management maturity and quality.
- Uplifted cybersecurity and risk maturity by reducing data leakage and data-handling issues while improving Security's ability to detect, respond, and mitigate threats more efficiently.

This transformation yielded significant positive impacts across the organization:

- 525% increase in Time to Insight
- 900% enhancement in first-party on-demand query response time
- 4,400% improvement in historical log query processing, driven by enhanced data management and trusted infrastructure

- 322% reduction in job processing time
- 626% enhancement in compute utilization

Gaining buy-in from product and data teams was straightforward. However, the challenge lay in advocating for offense-oriented data strategies while emphasizing data-centric defense protocols and gaining approval and support from privacy and security teams.

Once it was recognized that the new adaptable schema designs mitigated data leakage risks, improved data classification accuracy, and enhanced data lineage tracking, support cascaded across the defensive sister teams. The performance metrics realized by cybersecurity, CSIRT, threat detection teams, and other departments underscored the effectiveness of this balanced approach.

This example exemplifies how balancing data-driven offense, effective data management, infrastructure modernization, and comprehensive risk mitigation strategies amplifies value even for privacy and security teams, ensuring a holistic and robust data-centric approach.

This strategy required not only an investment in data, and technology – it also required people investment and a balanced approach. By creating a hiring strategy based on not only operational gaps, but existing skill gaps, we hired for long-term success. This included a significant investment in our data management, product, and data platform team to systematically manage relationships, experiences, data, risk, and our data-related infrastructure to meet business and trust needs.

AI was an aspect of our advanced analytics data strategy that supported real-time analytics, data scientists, and machine learning engineers with data, processes, and policies to ensure their success and focus.

Vitalizing an effective accountability model

Implementing a successful data and AI model hinges on the right accountability structure. A technology-only approach might lead to headline-making AI mishaps. Acknowledging the crucial role of data in AI functionality and embracing a Data by Design approach becomes indispensable. This approach optimizes resources, reduces costs, mitigates risks, and fuels proactive AI innovation.

Organization structures might vary, but the fundamental truth remains that data serves as the focal point, with AI acting as a new consumer and producer. Over 90%[10] of respondents from various organizations emphasized the importance of data protection and privacy in ensuring the trustworthiness and accountability of AI systems. Organizations lacking a CDAIO must consider appointing one. An exemplary executive accountability model embodies diverse roles like the following:

- **Board of Directors**: The board resembles composers and playwrights, setting the organizational tone and direction—the vision and guiding principles shaping the entire performance.

- **Chief Data & AI Officer (CDAIO)**: The CDAIO acts as the orchestra conductor, leading and coordinating various departments to perform cohesively. Like a maestro, they interpret the data strategy's musical score, ensuring harmonious execution of the musical data notes and tempo through the organization.

- **Chief Technology Officer (CTO)**: Like instrumentalists, the CTO provides the necessary technology infrastructure and tools, ensuring that each *instrument* (technology) produces the desired capabilities for effective performance. They operationalize tools and processes to make AI responsible as a service.

- **Chief Information Officer (CIO)**: Functions as the stage manager, orchestrating smooth transitions and information between the different lines of business, technology, and data.

- **Chief Information Security Officer (CISO)**: Serves as the guardian, ensuring the security and integrity of the organization's performance against potential disruptions and threats.

- **Chief Legal/Privacy Officer (CPO)**: Resembles an expert music critic and analyst, responsible for ensuring that AI initiatives comply with established legal and ethical guidelines, ensuring harmony between the music, organizational activities, and regulatory frameworks.

- **Chief Marketing Officer (CMO)**: The promoter of the event sets the tone, and intended outcome and spotlights the musicians or score. Often a consumer of AI services, the CMO will use AI to generate content for marketing purposes. As a part of the AI task force the CMO should help identify harm from non-performant pieces of AI to the brand.

90%

of respondents noted the importance of data protection and privacy for trustworthy and accountable AI

- **Chief Executive Officer (CEO):** The event manager ensures all the people, processes, and outcomes create a magical night of music in a wonderful venue with a full crowd. The CEO should ensure the accountability is clear, communicated, and that the various players understand their roles and responsibilities. They should be laser-focused on ensuring the CDAIO is set up for success.

Of course, there are many C-suite titles and various organization diagrams. All chief executives have a role when it comes to AI and data, as a consumer, a producer, and as a steward. The Chief Compliance Officer, Chief Finance Officer, Chief Operating Officer, and others should all be involved and informed of the outcomes of each step.

Establishing an AI task force

The establishment of an AI task force is a pivotal initiative in navigating the intricate landscape of AI. Led by the CDAIO, this cross-functional bridge (CISO, CIO, CTO, risk, privacy, and business teams) embodies a strategic cornerstone dedicated to steering the organization through the complexities of AI integration with proper balance. Its primary objective revolves around meticulously managing the AI trip and its risks, devising standardization best practices, and using cutting-edge technology to ensure the seamless and impactful integration of AI across operations.

> **“The AI task force should have dotted lines reporting to the data governance council, the risk council, and the CEO.”**

The AI task force should have dotted lines reporting to the data governance council, the risk council, and the CEO to ensure awareness, progress, and proper stakeholder awareness and buy-in, with the CDAIO representing the team's progress, roadblocks, and risks to the board. If you are in an organization that has an established ethics board (such as the institutional review board (IRB) in healthcare), the AI task force should have a dotted line there as well. This sounds complex, but AI is complex. A data quality issue, which is the purview of the data governance council, can then lead to a biased AI model, which might be tied to the IRB in healthcare or a legal risk being tracked by your risk teams.

At the forefront of the task force's mandate lies the meticulous evaluation of AI integration benefits and its potential risks. This involves conducting a comprehensive analysis of business and data readiness, the potential risks in deploying AI solutions, and the formulation of strategies to measure, mitigate, and monitor these risks effectively. Moreover, a paramount focus of the task force is to establish and uphold standardized best practices, data, and technology frameworks. By setting these foundations, the organization endeavors to streamline AI implementations, ensuring consistency and reliability in its applications.

Furthermore, ethical alignment and literacy are critical outcomes of the task force's purview. Emphasizing and enforcing ethical considerations in AI deployment remains integral, thereby aligning the organization's AI initiatives with ethical standards and guidelines. In parallel, the task force must maintain a laser focus on the ROI of AI endeavors. The task force rigorously evaluates the efficacy of AI initiatives, scrutinizing their impact on the organization's bottom line while strategically aligning AI deployments with tangible business outcomes.

By amalgamating a multifaceted approach encompassing business and data readiness, risk assessment, standardized practices, ethical alignment, and ROI scrutiny, the task force operates as a vanguard, steering organizations toward a responsible, efficient, and impactful AI-driven future. This is not a one-and-done activity; this function should be carried forward long after your initial AI implementations are complete and it should be integrated into your change management functions, becoming the ring that binds your strategies together, proactively addressing business, data, technology, and the evolving regulatory world together.

Step 2: Assessing business readiness

Embarking on the journey toward AI implementation demands an acute comprehension of your organization's business funnel, the maturity level of the supporting processes, and its data. This phase necessitates a meticulous evaluation of the operational, tactical, and strategic strata of your business operations, aiming to pinpoint areas with mature business and data processes that are ripe for AI integration and improvement. By using the various skill sets and specialty areas of the AI task force, you can combine business, data, technology, and risk frameworks into a new framework that defines, measures, and provides mitigation steps for all.

Understanding the organizational business process funnel

Begin by grasping the entirety of your business funnel, encompassing every facet from initial customer interaction, lead generation, and sales to service delivery and customer support. Each stage of this funnel holds the potential for AI augmentation, but not all may be immediately adaptable. Assessing the maturity of these processes is critical to discern where AI can be most seamlessly and effectively integrated.

Concentrate on areas demonstrating robust operational efficiency. These are sections where processes are well documented and established and exhibit a record of stability and efficacy. Operational effectiveness also implies a level of data maturity with consistent, measurable outputs and well-defined inputs. Such areas serve as fertile ground for AI implementation, providing a stable base for the introduction and scaling of innovative technologies. Only 35%[11] of CDOs feel they have "a lot" or "completely" enough resources to fulfill the requirements of clean data that it is highly accessible and reusable for their trajectory to AI adoption.

> "Only 35% of CDOs feel they have a lot or completely enough resources to fulfill the requirements of clean data that it is highly accessible and reusable for their trajectory to AI adoption."

Identifying AI-ready processes

Alongside operational soundness, evaluate the maturity of your data processes. This involves understanding data collection methods, management, analysis practices, and the quality of insights generated. A mature analytics setup will include data governance mechanisms, quality control measures, and a clear understanding of data lineage, laying a robust foundation for effective AI deployment.

Within your operationally mature and analytically robust processes, pinpoint those ready for automation. These are repetitive, rule-based processes with clearly defined outcomes. Automation-ready processes represent prime candidates for AI application, allowing for the direct utilization of AI technologies, such as machine learning and natural language processing, to enhance efficiency and precision.

Prioritizing based on business impact

As you identify mature areas, prioritize them based on their potential business impact. Factors such as volume of activity, revenue generation capacity, customer satisfaction, operational reliability, and costs should be considered. Concentrating on high-impact areas ensures that your AI initiatives deliver substantial value and contribute to long-term strategic objectives.

Engage stakeholders from diverse departments in the maturity assessment. Different teams offer unique insights into various business processes and data nuances. A collaborative approach ensures a holistic understanding of your business landscape and identifies areas where AI can yield the most significant benefits. Partnering with your risk management team to build quantitative or qualitative risk-to-benefit models will help with prioritization and making decisions.

Upskilling employees

Ensuring a human is present in the AI loop is vital. Engage employees from AI-ready functions to document processes and bridge data management gaps. Offer upskilling programs to empower employees with AI model auditing, training capabilities, or support roles, fostering a knowledgeable workforce capable of sustaining AI-driven transitions.

> **"The cultural lens cannot be ignored, as it is the root cause of many data failure points."**

Armed with a clear understanding of your mature business areas, you are equipped to advance to the subsequent stages of the AI journey. This exercise will give insights into not only business readiness but also potential areas for cultural fine-tuning. The cultural lens cannot be ignored, as it is the root cause of many data failure points. Initiating data rationalization and quality assessments is essential to ensure that your AI systems receive high-quality data inputs.

By meticulously identifying operationally mature segments within your business funnel, you establish a robust bedrock for AI implementation. This groundwork guarantees that your AI initiatives rest on stable, efficient, and impactful business processes, ensuring more successful outcomes and a smoother integration of AI into your organizational fabric and culture.

Step 3: Assessing data readiness

Data rationalization involves the systematic review, cleansing, and organization of your organization's data assets to bolster efficiency, curtail costs, and amplify data quality, accessibility, and reliability. This critical process involves purging unnecessary data (termed as redundant, obsolete, or trivial (ROT)), identifying valuable data based on relevance, accuracy, and business value, and aligning data initiatives with business strategies, metrics, objectives and key results (OKRs), and initiatives.

To execute a successful data rationalization project, a clear and defined focus is crucial, often established through a specific business use case with a well-defined scope and exit criteria. The involvement of a cross-functional team inclusive of key stakeholders such as C-suite sponsors, business operations, partner ecosystems, IT, and relevant business application and data teams is vital for success. Additionally, your data governance council plays a pivotal role in providing oversight and managing issues.

Importance and benefits of data rationalization

Data rationalization, coupled with data management maturity, enhances an organization's data environment. It is akin to conducting a detailed data audit, focusing on the data itself and the processes surrounding it. This process ensures optimized, comprehensible, and trustworthy data, elevating efficiency and scalability while mitigating risks associated with compliance and regulations—which is especially critical for AI consumption, where non-compliant, sensitive, or unethical data can lead to legal repercussions and trust issues.

Integrating data rationalization and maturity frameworks

Data management maturity frameworks, such as the EDM Council's Cloud Data Management Capability (CDMC)[12] framework or the Data Management Association's (DAMA's)[13] principles, complement data rationalization by providing structured methodologies and best practices. This synergistic approach not only ensures the optimal handling of specific data through rationalization audits but also maintains the overall data strategy, governance, processes, and infrastructure in line with industry standards.

Documenting and assessing data

Capture and comprehend the business process funnel, identify cross-functional touchpoints, key operational tasks, and decision accountability. As a reminder, not all AI is as risky as generative AI. If it is a non-generative AI implementation, then your rigor should be based on the risk of the AI solution. There are great standards for responsible AI data documentation, such as the Data Cards[14] framework:

> "Not all AI is as risky as generative AI."

- **Data and usage documentation**:
    - Note the underlying business applications, systems of records, source systems, data stores/lakes, and respective data owners and stewards.
    - Detail the critical business dimensions and metrics and their alignment to OKRs, linking them to reports, visualizations, data productions, decision points, and business strategy enablement.
    - Identify and document business logic, data quality rules, and taxonomy.
    - Categorize stored data according to standards such as ISO 19444 and ISO 27001 or ISO/IEC 22989, which establishes terminology for AI and describes AI concepts.
    - Define the company's role concerning data—whether as a processor, sub-processor, or controller.

    - Capture data quality process maturity and the overall data quality score.

- **Policy and life cycle documentation**:

    - Establish and document data policies and standards, covering access control, data categorization and classification, data handling, and retention policies.

    - Outline data life cycle specifics and the associated policies and data-handling requirements.

    - Document data change management processes and communication protocols, identifying any gaps.

- **Assessing data risk and accountability**:

    - Understand and define existing risk, geo-residency, and compliance landscapes related to data, such as GDPR, CCPA, and HIPPA.

    - Evaluate data in the context of new AI risk landscapes.

    - Assign accountable executives to a mitigation action plan (MAP).

    - Assess risks as blockers to AI implementation, or whether they can be handled post-implementation.

    - Update appropriate strategies, backlogs, and feature- or bug-tracking systems.

Navigating data quality and accountability

Data quality is a paramount concern for AI readiness. If data is not high quality or lacks repeatability, it is not ready for AI consumption. Addressing data quality can be a significant undertaking; IBM has estimated a $3.1 trillion[15] loss due to data quality issues in the US alone. In other words, data engineers, analysts, data scientists, and machine learning engineers spend most of their time finding or cleaning data as opposed to producing high-business value insights, and business teams spend a lot of time questioning data as opposed to making decisions from it.

$3.1 trillion

loss in the US due to data quality issues

Often, data quality issues boil down to one of three things: poor business processes, immature change management processes, and a lack of clear data accountability. Data, being a shared commodity, needs an accountable executive backed with the necessary resourcing and funding to ensure its effective management and usage. This includes focusing on well-known business processes, improving existing data quality, and mitigating new data quality risks introduced by AI.

Your data rationalization efforts are key to identifying areas needed for data change management, business rule standardization, or domain-specific accountability closures. This comprehensive approach ensures that your AI systems are powered by high-quality, necessary data, leading to effective and efficient outcomes. Reliable, clean, repeatable, and governed data form the foundation, while riskier data is introduced gradually, with close monitoring for quality, behavior, and ethical considerations.

In the realm of data, data quality issues often manifest in various forms, such as accuracy discrepancies or loss problems. However, one critical AI data quality concern is bias. Bias often stems from non-representative datasets or the absence of mechanisms to identify and rectify biases due to missing user attributes. Bias in AI occurs when algorithms produce results that systematically and unfairly discriminate against certain groups or individuals. Representative data refers to datasets that accurately mirror the diversity and characteristics of the population or user base they aim to represent. On the other hand, user-reflective data involves attributes that truly capture the spectrum of users' characteristics and behaviors. To mitigate bias, it is imperative to conduct a thorough risk assessment before AI implementation. This proactive approach helps anticipate potential biases in the AI system and enables the implementation of corrective measures to ensure fairness, accuracy, and ethical use of the AI model.

Step 4: Understanding the risk landscape

In the ongoing journey to incorporate AI into your organizational structure, it's vital to grasp the intricate web of risks it entails. Introducing AI without a comprehensive understanding of existing data management maturity and potential risk factors is akin to bringing in a poorly behaved AI entity.

Unique risks introduced by AI and potential mitigations

As with every advancement, AI has risks. As the tech giants battle for AI dominance, policymakers and regulators will try to keep up the pace. The recently released US AI Executive Order[16] and the EU AI Policy[17] are great regulatory starts, but they still ignore that *data* elephant in the room. Let's explore some of the new risks that AI introduces and discuss how a Data by Design approach can mitigate these risks while preparing you for the data regulations to come.

Risks introduced by AI	Design approach to mitigate risk
Poor Data by Design as a bad actor Organizations rushing into AI adoption can inadvertently harm themselves by neglecting proper data practices.	• Establish a Data by Design framework and training program to ensure employees and customers understand the fundamentals of data design. • Implement robust metadata tagging and data lineage services to improve data change management and data risk management. • Enhance cybersecurity and regulatory compliance efforts, laying a foundation for complicated AI use case regulations.
AI bias The data used to train AI can significantly impact its outputs and behavior. AI bias can lead to systematic and unfair prejudices, reflecting biases in the training data, the algorithm design, or the engineers' subjective decisions.	• Employ generative AI techniques to balance biased data, using demographic information to assess its alignment with the organization's customer base. • Define when bias is acceptable for business success. For example, many companies intentionally target specific consumers or customer types and use bias to drive the brand.
AI quality Ensuring the quality of AI outputs is paramount. Maintaining high-quality, repeatable, fit-for-use data is key to ensuring AI quality.	• Monitor AI performance using statistical measures to meet a performance bar before release. • Implement formal processes for model retraining in areas where performance metrics are not reliable. • Establish fast feedback loops with customers to spot areas where statistical measures might be unreliable.
AI ethics AI ethics encompasses considerations of bias, privacy, equality, and even issues such as copyright infringement,[18] plagiarism, and intellectual property (IP).[19]	• Adopt a Data by Design framework and publishing an ethical AI policy ensures data collection and utilization align with your company's values and responsible AI practices. • Hire an ethicist and follow established guidelines such as UNESCO's Ethics of Artificial Intelligence[20] framework.

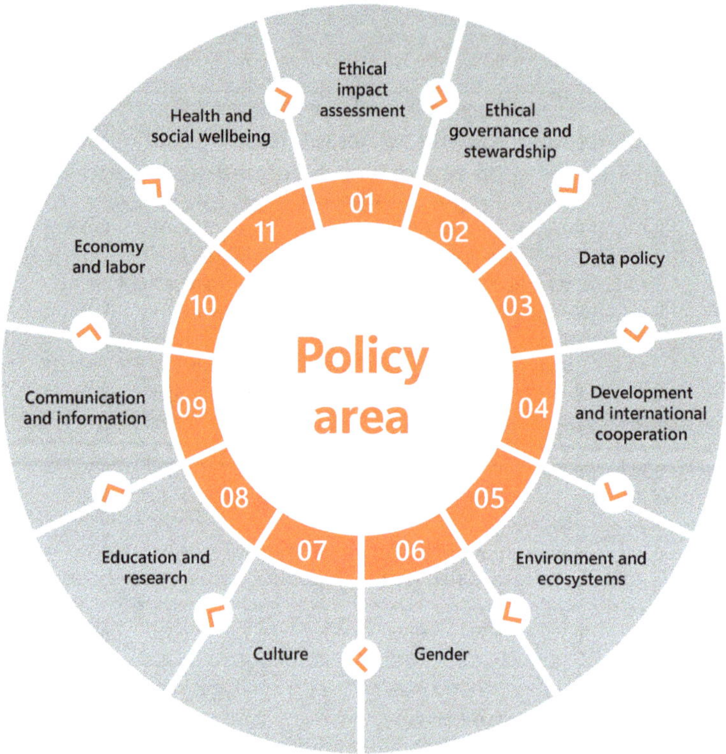

A deep dive into AI-related IP risk

Within applications and software, logging, instrumentation, and event practices serve multiple purposes. Data capture is essential to guaranteeing user experience, performance optimization, debugging, system reliability, and security. The level of risk often hinges on how a software engineer defines and executes the automation of these event captures, or how users input personal or confidential information, potentially leading to data leaks. This leakage is commonly rooted in inadequate data capture design and a lack of clear data-handling protocols or inadequate training.

The necessity of data capture to ensure seamless service, coupled with the evolving AI transformation among software and service providers, and the advancement of AI copilots, introduces new concerns related to IP. This was exemplified by the introduction of Zoom's AI copilot[21] this year, and the lack of clarity as to how the copilot models are trained. As AI integrations can span voice, facial/video recognition, or written language entry points, there are new risks associated with choosing your internal infrastructure services and how they collect, aggregate, and utilize service events. While not all executives need to understand these intricacies, the AI task force and the board do.

While organizations have long been aware of data quality risks, they often defer addressing them due to the high costs associated with correcting business processes, cleaning up data, or avoiding internal politics. However, the advent of AI has transformed data quality from a *nice to have* into an imperative *must-do*. Many of the new risks introduced by AI do not necessarily require a legal or regulatory framework to proactively manage and mitigate; instead, they can be effectively approached through a strategic risk lens.

The power of data risk management

The development of a robust data risk management program is essential for addressing immediate risks and building a resilient organization that is equipped to navigate and thrive amid the new challenges AI brings.

By prioritizing data management maturity and aligning it with broader cybersecurity and privacy efforts, organizations can ensure a balanced, ethical, and effective AI implementation while still deriving data decision-making and monetization opportunities.

> **"In 2020 alone, data breaches exposed over 36 billion records globally."**

Breaches, privacy penalties, and geo-residency mandates underscore the significance of data as an asset. In a digital, and now the AI era, it is data that will delineate the success stories from the failures. Statistics highlight the gravity of these risks; for instance, in 2020 alone, data breaches exposed over 36 billion[22] records globally, indicating the pervasive threat landscape faced by organizations. Many companies consider cybersecurity, privacy, and customer growth as top-risk areas; however, it is data that fuels these risk areas.

A dedicated data risk management program will address the root cause and any missing foundations of your cyber and privacy risks while also fueling business growth, missed opportunity, M&A integration, and ROI risks. Companies that prioritize cybersecurity, aligning with the National Institute of Standards and Technology's (NIST's) Cybersecurity Framework,[23] must equally invest in enhancing data management maturity. Studies indicate that investing in data management maturity contributes to over 40% of the NIST uplift, emphasizing its critical role in bolstering overall security measures.

Step 5: Data roadmap – using generative AI to uplift readiness

As organizations shift to integrating generative AI into operational frameworks to significantly enhance implementation success, the question arises: how can they safely use generative AI to immediately generate ROI? One solution is to create a dedicated sandbox environment tailored for content generation and the development of custom large language models (LLMs) and language graphs specific to the organization. This approach allows for immediate enhancement of existing data strategies, processes, and AI tactical roadmaps, while consolidating insights gleaned from comprehensive business, data, and risk assessments.

> "91% of C-suite respondents believe AI adoption will empower them to surpass competitors and expand market influence."

Isolating risks with sandboxes for content generation

The creation of an isolated sandbox environment for generative AI content generation is useful. This sandbox functions as a secure haven where AI algorithms can explore and generate content without interfering with operational data or processes. It allows organizations to experiment, refine, and optimize custom AI models and algorithms, ensuring they align with the desired outcomes and organizational objectives. Moreover, this controlled space facilitates the analysis and validation of AI-generated content, ensuring its relevance, accuracy, and compliance with established standards before its implementation in live environments.

Developing custom AI models such as LLMs or even integrating LLMs with knowledge graphs can unlock new ways to manage risks. These models can fine-tune AI capabilities to comprehend and generate content specific to the organization's domain, optimizing accuracy and relevance. By training LLMs on proprietary data sources and industry-specific knowledge, organizations can harness AI's potential to a greater extent, enabling it to understand nuances, language variations, relationship patterns, and context unique to their operations.

Augmenting data strategy and tactical roadmaps

The insights gathered from extensive business, data, and risk assessments serve as the cornerstone for crafting strategic roadmaps fortified by the capabilities of generative AI. These findings function as guiding beacons, steering the tactical integration of AI into current workflows and operational frameworks. By harnessing generative AI as an augmentation layer on top of existing data strategies, organizations gain the means to address identified gaps highlighted in the assessments, ensuring smoother transitions within operations and the optimization of processes.

The prevalent belief in the business world is that AI adoption will lead to a decisive competitive edge. A recent Forbes Insights survey revealed that 91%[24] of C-suite respondents believe AI adoption will empower them to surpass competitors and expand market influence.

However, for successful machine learning and AI generation, data serves as the essential fuel—AI consumes data, relying solely on a steady supply of high-quality, consistent data to function optimally.

Regrettably, many companies fall short in this regard. Merely 12% of executives feel their organizations have established or are executing a comprehensive, company-wide strategy. Shockingly, 80% of executives assert that only a minimal percentage of data is discoverable or available for sharing within their company.

Initiating the journey toward an AI-driven future demands a forward-thinking, comprehensive enterprise-wide data strategy intricately aligned with the overarching business strategy. If an organization lacks a coherent data strategy, it is time for a fundamental reprioritization, rallying all stakeholders and reframing the perspective on data. Instead of perceiving data as a mere operational cost center, it is crucial to shift the narrative, embracing data as a critical asset. This shift in perspective is pivotal in unleashing the true potential of data as a strategic asset within organizations.

Using AI-generated content to update and augment your data management services can fast-track your enterprise maturity and your data strategy efforts. By mapping the data, data processes, and data initiatives to your business strategies and overlaying this with the findings, content can be used to quantify business value of data. You can automate updates of your data catalog and business glossary and augment your data observation systems with this meaningful information.

Augmenting data analytics workflows with generative AI

The strategic integration of generative AI into established data analytics workflows represents a pivotal step in optimizing operational efficiency and accelerating the time to valuable insights. Notably, studies highlight that 54%[25] of companies report noticeable cost and operation efficiencies upon AI implementation. Aligning generative AI harmoniously with existing analytics workflows serves to streamline processes, elevate data interpretation capabilities, and significantly augment the speed and precision of decision-making.

54%

companies report cost and operation efficiencies upon AI implementation

To ensure the success of AI integration, a phased approach is paramount, initiating pilot projects to validate efficacy before scaling across the organization. This meticulous strategy mitigates risk and facilitates a smooth transition while allowing for the upskilling of employees in the process. One effective method involves utilizing existing business processes with their predefined OKRs alongside established decision-making patterns as a testing ground for AI implementation. By phasing the introduction of AI alongside proven analytics processes, organizations minimize risks and operational costs while simultaneously fostering employee growth and expertise. The value of the augmentation is as follows:

- **Operational efficiency**: Integrating generative AI streamlines processes within data analytics workflows, automating repetitive tasks and expediting data analysis. This efficiency translates to reduced manual effort, optimized resource allocation, and faster delivery of insights.
- **Improved time to insights**: Generative AI accelerates the analysis of vast datasets, enabling quick extraction of meaningful insights. This agility in data processing expedites decision-making timelines, empowering organizations to respond swiftly to dynamic market conditions.
- **Agility in decision-making**: The infusion of generative AI into analytics workflows empowers decision-makers with more comprehensive and granular insights. This agility fosters adaptive decision-making, enabling organizations to pivot swiftly and make informed choices in real time. This leads to improved market opportunity and risk mitigation.

Moreover, the application of a natural language layer further democratizes data access, ensuring a data-driven culture by assuring data accuracy, reliability, and impact across diverse organization functions. The integration of generative AI with a natural language layer not only enhances analytics workflows but also democratizes data accessibility, enabling employees at all levels to use data effectively and fostering a culture of data-driven decision-making across the organization.

Assisted training using LLMs to elevate data quality and comprehension signifies a significant leap forward. Models such as GPT-3 and GPT-4, boasting over 175 billion parameters, stand as key players in grasping data by generating text in human language. The capabilities of generative AI, particularly LLMs, extend beyond data comprehension; they actively contribute to interpreting and purifying data, thereby fostering an enriched understanding.

These AI-driven tools contribute to enhancing business acumen by simplifying complex data into actionable insights. Additionally, they fortify business fluency and data literacy within organizations, empowering teams to make informed decisions grounded in a deeper understanding of the business and data landscape. The integration of LLMs significantly streamlines this process while enhancing output quality. The model interprets nuanced sentiments within feedback, identifies customer preferences, and uncovers emerging trends. It distinguishes positive and negative sentiments in reviews, identifies recurring keywords denoting customer satisfaction or discontent, and spotlights specific product attributes garnering attention.

Uplifting compliance, regulation, and security

In today's global landscape, ensuring adherence to data regulations and compliance standards is paramount. With over 100+ AI regulations in existence globally and stringent data protection laws in over 60 countries, such as GDPR[26] in the EU and the CCPA[27] in California, the focus on safeguarding individual privacy rights is pronounced. Non-compliance incurs significant fines, as evidenced by tech giants such as Meta (formerly Facebook) and Google facing penalties for privacy and data-handling breaches. For instance, the Irish Data Protection Commission fined Meta €1.2 billion[28] for mishandling personal data during US and EU data transfers, violating GDPR regulation, and tech giant Google received penalties amounting to €50 million[29] imposed by France's data regulator for GDPR non-compliance. Despite the awareness of regulations, a limited percentage of companies feel they are GDPR- or CCPA-compliant, emphasizing the high stakes of data, privacy compliance, and its costs.

"As of 2023, there are 166 privacy regulations and 22 bills worldwide."

As of 2023, there are 166 privacy regulations and 22 bills worldwide, with AI's advancement posting new complexities requiring intricate data and privacy configurations. Generative AI becomes instrumental in aiding compliance efforts by enabling internal data examination, policy assessment, control monitoring, and data life cycle supervision. The capability to scan, communicate, quantify, and address risks is invaluable. Furthermore, AI facilitates generating data subsets that align with regional regulations or compliance controls.

This is crucial as organizations grapple with data residency complexities while training AI models.

The ability to construct datasets adhering to diverse privacy regulations across geographical regions is substantial. Generative AI enables businesses to simulate datasets meeting GDPR's stringent standards within the EU or the CCPA regulation in California. This ensures AI models are trained on data subsets compliant with specific privacy laws and regulatory needs. This capability is key to mitigating non-compliance risks and hefty fines and safeguarding brand trust. Once established, this future-state approach can be utilized to monitor existing datasets against the same compliance logic.

Utilizing findings for communication, training, and process materials

The valuable insights harvested from assessments serve as a wellspring for crafting communication strategies and training content and creating missing process materials. Generative AI, when employed tactically, aids in generating tailored communication materials, training modules, change management materials, and process documentation aligned with organizational objectives. By synthesizing complex findings into accessible and actionable content, generative AI becomes instrumental in fostering a deep understanding of operational changes among stakeholders, accelerating impact assessments and training initiatives and streamlining process documentation.

Step 6: Embracing the secret sauce – humanism and digital empathy

In the quest to integrate AI into organizational frameworks, it's imperative to bring employees and customers along on this transformative journey. Organization create an employee development and risk plan specific to the AI journey, outlining the importance of using resources to navigate AI readiness effectively.

Developing employees and retention risk management

As organizations embrace the AI journey, a robust employee development and risk plan becomes a cornerstone for success. This plan aims to upskill and redeploy employees, using existing resources to usher in a culture of AI readiness:

- **Upskilling for human involvement in AI models**: Employees can shift roles to become the humans in the loop, actively involved in training AI models and monitoring their outcomes. This role focuses on guiding AI systems, ensuring ethical and unbiased outputs.

> "As organizations embrace the AI journey, a robust employee development and risk plan becomes a cornerstone for success."

- **Transitioning to drive business process and data maturity**: Redeploying resources to the next business funnel stage of the data flow allows them to drive business processes. This involves fostering data maturity to expedite AI readiness. Additionally, training these individuals as AI *trains the trainers* equips them to handle AI-related training, communications, and operational monitoring for future stages.

- **Focusing on creativity and new business strategy**: Employees redeployed in this domain channel their expertise toward fostering creativity and devising new business strategies that align with AI integration. Encouraging innovative thinking and strategic vision becomes a core aspect of this role.

Central to the AI journey is the integration of business, data, technology, risk management, and empathy. Upskilling employees with business acumen, data literacy, risk understanding, critical thinking, and ethical considerations is key.

Understanding digital empathy

Digital empathy represents the vital link between customers and AI-driven systems, providing a comprehensive understanding of customer sentiments and expectations. As such, it is not just a customer service approach; it is a fundamental tool in managing long-term AI bias and risks, laying the foundation for ethical and responsible AI:

- **Long-term AI bias and risk management**: About 85%[30] of AI models have been found to exhibit some form of bias. By adopting a digital empathy approach, organizations can better find AI bias and risks beyond just statistics and math. Understanding customer needs and emotions helps in recognizing potential biases that might arise from historical data or algorithmic decisions. Addressing biases becomes an ongoing process rooted in empathetic understanding and continuous assessment.

> "About 85% of AI models have been found to exhibit some form of bias."

- **Ethical inquiry at the onset of the AI journey**: Digital empathy empowers organizations to ask critical bias and ethical questions about their data and its potential utilization as they embark on their AI journey. For instance:

- **Bias questions**:

    - Is our historical data representative of diverse demographics?
    - Are there inherent biases in the data collection process?
    - Does our dataset include a sufficient representation of minority populations or demographics?
    - Are there any historical biases that might skew our AI's decision-making process?

- **Ethical questions**:
    - How might this AI solution impact different customer groups?
    - Are there potential unintended consequences or ethical dilemmas that might arise from its deployment?
    - Are there privacy concerns or ethical implications in using certain types of data to train our AI models?

In summary, fostering a culture of humanism and digital empathy while upskilling employees is not just about customer service—it's a strategic approach to managing AI bias and risks. Using digital empathy ensures that AI systems are designed and implemented with a deep understanding of customer emotions, needs, and ethical considerations, leading to the creation of customer-centric and ethically sound AI implementations. This approach prepares employees to effectively operate in a data-driven AI environment while continuously assessing and refining AI systems to mitigate biases and uphold ethical standards.

Step 7: Implementing an AI Data by Design program

Data by Design represents an approach that integrates data management, data quality, ethics, privacy, and security considerations right from the outset of any data-related architecture, engineering, analytics, process, or system implementation. It goes beyond mere compliance, aiming to infuse data management, quality, linkability, and usage with ethical principles and secure practices into the very fabric of how data is developed, managed, accessed, and utilized. Data by Design ensures that your organization's data strategy is aligned with business goals, significantly improving the ROI of your data. Keeping this in mind, 44%[31] of organizations are working to embed AI into current applications and processes and two-thirds of companies are already or are planning to apply AI to their sustainability-related goals.

A robust Data by Design framework

A Data by Design framework should encompass the following:

- **Ethics by design**: Embedding ethical considerations into the entire data life cycle is fundamental. This includes assessing data collection practices, ensuring ethical sourcing, establishing transparent processes for data use, and understanding the potential impact on stakeholders.

- **Privacy and security by design**: Integrating robust privacy and security measures into the core of data practices is paramount. This involves encrypting sensitive information, implementing access controls, and ensuring compliance with relevant privacy laws or regulations. The use of the previously discussed data categories will dramatically improve these risk areas.

- **Streamlined approaches**: Rather than disparate, disjointed reviews of data processes, a cohesive Data by Design framework creates a unified lens for evaluating data-related strategies. This consolidated approach mitigates the risk of missing gaps or inconsistencies, enhancing overall data integrity and trustworthiness.

- **Business strategy enablement**: Data by Design ensures that data strategies are directly aligned with business objectives, driving value creation and strategic decision-making. It allows organizations to harness the full potential of their data assets in support of business goals.

- **Enhanced data quality and linkability**: Around 76% of consumers are concerned with misinformation from AI tools and 44% believe there is a stark difference between human-based generated content and the one generated by chatbots.[32] By embedding data quality measures within the design process, Data by Design significantly improves the reliability, consistency, and linkability of data across various business functions. This ensures data is readily available, accurate, and accessible for strategic use.

> **"76% of consumers are concerned with misinformation from AI tools and 44% believe there is a stark difference between human-based generated content and the one generated by chatbots."**

- **Ethics-infused data architecture and engineering**: Data architecture and engineering practices are foundational in modeling for ethics by design. This involves setting up architectures that proactively identify and address ethical concerns, ensuring that data is responsibly handled and utilized.

- **Data-first mentality**: The traditional approach of waiting until data reaches certain stages or applications before managing risks is inefficient. Data by Design advocates for a *shift-left* methodology, embedding risk management measures at the earliest stages of data processes, from ingestion to modeling.

Use Data by Design principles to customize your specific data-first framework, training, and communications plans. An example principle looks like this.

Implementing a Data by Design approach optimizes operational efficiency, enhances data quality, ensures alignment with business strategy, and significantly reduces risks associated with both the offensive and defensive landscapes of a company. It ensures that the data entering your systems is managed responsibly, securing it from potential threats or misuse from the outset, while also empowering its strategic utilization for business growth and decision-making:

- **Ethics infusion**: Ethical considerations are integral to every stage of data handling, ensuring responsible and transparent data practices.

- **Privacy protection**: Implement robust privacy measures to safeguard sensitive and personal information from unauthorized access or use.
- **Security integration**: Embed security protocols and measures into data systems to protect against breaches, cyber threats, and data vulnerabilities.
- **Early risk management**: Proactively identify and mitigate risks at the early stages of data processes, advocating a shift-left approach.
- **Alignment with business objectives**: Ensure that data strategies are aligned with organizational goals and contribute to business value.
- **Consistency and linkability**: Focus on maintaining consistent, accurate, and interconnected data across different applications and systems.
- **Transparent data governance**: Clearly define and enforce data governance policies, roles, and responsibilities throughout the data life cycle.
- **Compliance adherence**: Commit to adhering to legal and regulatory requirements governing data handling, processing, and storage.
- **Life cycle approach**: Embrace a holistic view of data, considering its entire life cycle from acquisition to disposal or archival.

- **Continuous improvement**: Encourage a culture of ongoing evaluation, learning, and refinement in data practices for continual enhancement.

Continuous feedback and improvement

This comprehensive approach involves establishing a feedback, monitoring, and improvement system that not only oversees the initiatives but also evaluates their impact. Measuring business value, strategy enhancement, risks, operational efficiency, employee and customer sentiment, and the effectiveness of training programs becomes imperative. Just as you review your business strategy's performance, the continuous assessment and refinement of data strategies, Data by Design practices, and AI implementations are vital for sustained success.

Furthermore, understanding that Data by Design and AI initiatives are iterative processes helps in creating a connected tissue within your organization. They necessitate a monitoring framework that provides actionable insights, allowing for real-time adjustments and improvements. Building this infrastructure for ongoing assessment aligns with the dynamic nature of these initiatives, fostering an environment of adaptability and growth.

> **"Understanding that Data by Design and AI initiatives are iterative processes helps in creating a connected tissue within your organization."**

To reinforce this initiative, collaboration between the CDAIO, the CISO, the Chief Legal/Privacy Officer, and the Chief People Officer is pivotal. This collaboration can strategize short-term and comprehensive long-term education plans that integrate data literacy, ethical practices, privacy protocols, security measures, and risk awareness into the organizational culture.

Breaking down these concepts and processes and seamlessly embedding them into application, system, infrastructure, data, analytics, and AI engineering processes is the cornerstone of success. This integration ensures that Data by Design and AI principles are not siloed efforts but rather interwoven throughout the organizational framework, ingrained in its cultural DNA for sustained evolution and improvement.

Real-world AI success cases

In the realm of retail and customer service, personalizing the customer experience has become a key differentiator. Advanced AI and machine learning technologies enable businesses to analyze customer data and provide personalized recommendations and services. This not only enhances the customer experience but also drives business value by increasing customer loyalty and sales. The global artificial intelligence market size is projected to expand at a compound annual growth rate (CAGR) of 37.3% from 2023 to 2030. It is projected to reach $1,811.8 billion by 2030.[33]

Case study: Starbucks – personalizing coffee encounters with AI

Starbucks, an international coffeehouse chain, is renowned for its commitment to customer service and innovation. Recognizing the potential of AI to further personalize the customer experience, Starbucks implemented an AI-driven system called Deep Brew.[34] With Deep Brew, Starbucks to:

- **Enable AI-powered recommendations**: Deep Brew was an initiative that included various AI technologies to enhance customer and partner experiences. One of its key features was personalization recommendations. The system would analyze a customer's previous orders, time of day, weather, and local store inventory to suggest items they might enjoy.

- **Improve operational efficiency**: Beyond personalization, the AI was built to assist in inventory engagement, staffing decisions, and predicting the necessary quantities of ingredients, thereby improving operational efficiency.

The impact of Deep Brew was notable, including the following:

Increased sales

- **Increased sales**: By offering personalized options, Starbucks not only enhanced the customer experience but also saw a direct impact on sales. Customers were more likely to purchase suggested items that aligned with their tastes and habits.

Improved customer engagement

- **Improved customer engagement**: The personalized experience led to increased customer engagement and loyalty. Customers enjoyed a tailored experience that remembered their preferences and suggested new types of coffee they were more likely to enjoy.

Starbucks has been able to benefit from their robust rewards program, fostering long-term brand loyalty that drives higher sales volume. Their Deep Brew analytics platform allows targeted incentives for specific customer segments. This strategy has been successful, with a 13% year-over-year increase in their U.S. rewards program active membership base, reaching 34.3 million (a gain of roughly 4 million new members).[35]

Case study: UPS – optimizing deliveries with generative AI

In the logistics and supply chain industry, efficiency and timely delivery are crucial. Generative AI has emerged as a powerful tool for enhancing these aspects by predicting and optimizing routes and inventory, leading to reduced costs and improved delivery times.

UPS, a global leader in logistics, has been at the forefront of adopting innovative technologies to optimize its delivery and operational processes. The company has implemented an advanced AI program named ORION (On-Road Integrated Optimization and Navigation)[36] to enhance its delivery routes. ORION's mission is as follows:

- **Provide predictive analytics for route optimization**: ORION uses generative AI and advanced algorithms to analyze delivery routes in real time, considering factors such as traffic, weather, and the location of the packages in the vehicle. Using this data, it then generates the most efficient route for the drivers.
- **Establish dynamic inventory management**: Alongside route optimization, AI tools are used to predict inventory levels, helping to streamline warehouse operations, ensuring the goods are in the right place at the right time.

ORION's impact has been significant, in that the following was achieved:

- **Reduced delivery times**: By optimizing routes, UPS significantly reduced its delivery times. While the exact percentage may vary, the use of ORION led to a reduction in miles driven per driver, saving millions of gallons of fuel annually. This has had a positive environmental impact while also reducing delivery times.

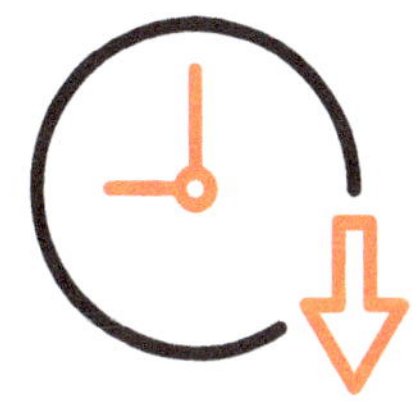

Reduced delivery time

- **Decreased operational costs**: The efficiency gained through better route planning and inventory management decreased operational costs. UPS reported millions of dollars in savings due to reduced fuel consumption and improved operational efficiency.

Decreased operational costs

ORION is a real-world example of the potential of generative AI to transform supply chain management. The technology not only enhances operational efficiency but also contributes to significant cost savings and service improvements. Dynamic ORION is an upgrade to the ORION technology that has enabled UPS in reducing driver routes by an average of two to four miles per driver. Whereas, the original ORION implementation resulted in a reduction of eight miles per driver. The new system is already being used by 97% of the van fleet that uses ORION.[37]

Case study: Netflix personalizing user engagement with generative AI

The marketing industry constantly seeks innovative ways to capture attention and engage audiences. Generative AI has become a revolutionary tool in this space, enabling the creation of personalized and compelling content at scale, which can significantly enhance campaign effectiveness.

Netflix, a leading global entertainment service, has pioneered the use of AI and machine learning to revolutionize how users engage with content. While it is not a traditional marketing agency, its innovative use of AI for personalization serves as an influential case study in the marketing domain for the following:

- **Generative AI for personalized thumbnails**: Netflix uses generative AI to create and test different thumbnails for its shows and movies. The AI analyzes individual viewing habits and preferences to generate and display the thumbnails most likely to engage that specific user.

- **Tailored content and recommendations**: Beyond thumbnails, Netflix's AI algorithms analyze vast amounts of data to personalize and generate content recommendations, ensuring users are presented with shows and movies that align with their tastes.

The impact has been huge; the innovative approach saw business impact via the following:

- **Increased click-through rates**: By presenting personalized thumbnails, Netflix experienced a significant increase in click-through rates. While Netflix has not publicly disclosed the exact number, personalized images have been proven to improve user engagement.

Increased
click-through rates

- **Improved conversion rates**: The tailored experience does not just stop at clicks. By providing highly relevant content suggestions, Netflix has seen improvements in viewer retention and conversion rates. This translates to improved prolonged subscriptions and higher customer satisfaction.

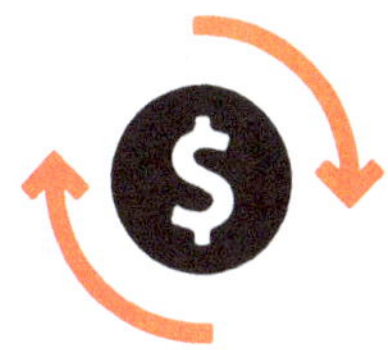

Improved
conversion rates

- **Algorithm monetization**: The Netflix models were so successful that they not only led to an improved customer experience and retention but also to the monetization of the algorithm itself.

Improved
algorithmic monetization

Netflix has discussed its use of AI and personalization techniques in various technology blogs, interviews, and articles. Detailed insights into how Netflix uses generative AI for personalization and its impact on user engagement can be found on its technology blog[38] and in industry analysis reports. Generative AI can be used in innovative ways to revolutionize marketing strategies and content creation, leading to significant improvements in engagement metrics. More than 80% of the content watched on Netflix is discovered through its recommendation system.[39]

Case study: Siemens streamlines operations with generative AI

Manufacturing firms are increasingly turning to generative AI to enhance operational efficiency, particularly through predictive maintenance paired with generative AI. By predicting equipment failures before they occur, companies can schedule timely maintenance, reduce downtime, and increase overall productivity.

Siemens, a global powerhouse in electronics and industrial engineering, has been implementing generative AI in its manufacturing processes to revolutionize predictive maintenance. The company's use of AI in its operations serves as a robust example of enhancing efficiency and productivity in the manufacturing sector in the following ways:

- **Employing generative AI for predictive maintenance**: Siemens employs generative AI algorithms to monitor the conditions of equipment and predict when maintenance should be performed. This approach is based on real-time data from sensors and historical data analysis, enabling the system to identify patterns that precede equipment failures.

- **Optimizing maintenance schedules**: The AI system not only predicts potential issues but also suggests optimal times for maintenance, thereby minimizing disruptions and ensuring a smooth manufacturing process.

As a result, Siemens has realized significant value, including the following:

- **Reduced equipment downtime**: With a proactive maintenance strategy powered by generative AI, Siemens has reported a reduction in equipment downtime and a significant decrease in unplanned outages.

Reduced
equipment downtime

- **Increased overall productivity**: By ensuring equipment runs reliably and maintenance is conducted efficiently, Siemens has seen an improvement in overall productivity.

Increased
overall productivity

Siemens has openly discussed its digitalization and AI efforts in various press releases, reports, and interviews and on their official website.[40] Siemens' use of data and generative AI is a notable example of the power of generative AI in the manufacturing sector.

Recommendations and best practices

These studies and outcome examples underscore the tangible impact and transformative potential of generative AI paired with data and analytics across diverse industries. From revolutionizing customer experiences and supply chain management to transforming marketing strategies and enhancing operational efficiency, generative AI has emerged as a catalyst for innovation, driving substantial improvements in key business metrics and outcomes.

Below are some recommended best practices for organizations looking to implement generative AI effectively:

- Foster a culture of continuous learning, digital empathy, and upskilling to empower employees in using generative AI.
- Embrace pilot projects to validate the efficacy of AI applications before widespread implementation.
- Collaborate across departments to ensure seamless integration and the alignment of AI initiatives with corporate strategies and organizational goals.
- Prioritize Data by Design throughout AI implementation processes.

Now that you've grasped the fundamentals of generative AI, the crucial reliance on data, and the transformative potential it holds for your business, let's delve into the future of generative AI in data and analytics.

The future of generative AI in data and analytics

The future of generative AI in data and analytics is a landscape defined by its innovative potential, transformative impact, and role in shaping the next phase of data-driven decision-making. Generative AI is poised to lead the charge in transforming how organizations handle data. The future will witness a surge in innovative applications powered by generative AI, enabling the creation of synthetic data, augmentation of existing datasets, and development of more robust predictive models. Expenditures by enterprises on Generative AI services, software, and infrastructure are projected to surge from $16 billion in 2023 to $143 billion by 2027.[41]

> "Expenditures by enterprises on Generative AI services, software, and infrastructure are projected to surge from $16 billion in 2023 to $143 billion by 2027."

Advancements toward AGI

The pursuit of AGI, with the aim to create AI systems capable of understanding, learning, and applying knowledge across diverse domains, is a focal point. The quest for AGI marks a shift from specialized AI toward more adaptable and autonomous systems. Additionally, the aspiration for sentient AI, capable of consciousness and self-awareness, fuels speculative discussions about the nature of AI's future capabilities.

The rise of personal AI devices and RAG models

The proliferation of personal AI copilots and then devices mark a significant shift in everyday interactions and individual efficiency. These devices, incorporating conversational AI tailored to specific preferences, are reshaping task management, information accessibility, and communication for individuals. Recent innovations, such as retrieval-augmented generation (RAG) models, have notably advanced AI's capacity to comprehend and produce responses resembling human-like interactions, further amplifying its effectiveness within personal devices.

LLMs become world language models with knowledge graphs

LLMs evolving to world language models with integrated knowledge graphs are poised to revolutionize information processing and understanding. Combining LLMs into multilingual models with structured graph data will enable a deeper comprehension of context, relationships, and complex queries, leading to more sophisticated and accurate AI applications across industries and society as a whole.

Emergence of intelligent applications

The integration of AI into applications across diverse sectors, from education to healthcare, will not only reshape employee, user, and customer experiences; it will also simplify technology infrastructure stacks and dramatically reduce risks. Intelligent applications powered by AI-defined business semantic layers, essentially enabling business logic and decision workflows to be applied directly to data, will dramatically reduce the need for business applications instead of building intelligent application layers directly on data lakes and stores, while still enabling a human in the loop with knowledge graph-based interfaces to ensure semantic logic, model training, and behavioral outcomes.

AI-led classrooms, healthcare, and social interactions

AI's integration into classrooms is transforming educational experiences, enabling personalized learning paths, adaptive assessments, and intuitive feedback mechanisms. Similarly, in healthcare, AI-led diagnostics, personalized treatment plans, and predictive analytics are augmenting medical professionals' capabilities. Moreover, AI-driven social interaction platforms are reshaping how people connect, fostering friendships and providing support.

The future of AI is multifaceted, presenting opportunities and challenges as technology continues to evolve. The ethical considerations surrounding AI's advanced capabilities, its impact on privacy, bias mitigation, and its role in society will require careful navigation and proactive governance. Nonetheless, AI's potential to revolutionize industries, elevate human potential, and reshape everyday life is immense and promises a future of unprecedented innovation and possibilities.

> "The next generation of analytics will be characterized by generative AI's integration into various facets of data management, analysis, and interpretation."

Impact of generative AI on data-driven decision-making

Generative AI's influence on data-driven decision-making will be profound. Its ability to generate synthetic data that mirrors real-world scenarios without compromising privacy or security will unlock new avenues for experimentation and testing. This will enhance decision-making processes, fuel creativity in problem-solving, and foster a deeper understanding of complex datasets, empowering organizations to make more informed and impactful decisions.

The next generation of analytics will be characterized by generative AI's integration into various facets of data management, analysis, and interpretation. It will redefine how organizations interact with and use data. From generating large-scale datasets for training AI models to creating realistic simulations for testing, generative AI will become an indispensable tool for future analytics professionals.

The road ahead: Embracing the AI revolution

Embracing the AI revolution involves adapting to the changing landscape by fostering a culture of innovation, continuous learning, and agile adaptation. Organizations must embrace generative AI as a catalyst for growth and evolution. This entails investment in research and development, nurturing talent capable of harnessing the technology, and establishing robust governance frameworks that ensure ethical and responsible AI usage.

Key takeaways for board members and executives

Executives navigating the future of generative AI in data and analytics must prioritize a few key takeaways:

- **Modernize your board**: Equip your board with knowledge about the impact and potential of generative AI, fostering a tech-savvy and forward-thinking governance approach, and invest in a CDAIO.
- **Embrace Data by Design**: Implement a proactive data strategy that integrates ethics, privacy, and security from the outset to optimize operations and mitigate risks.
- **Prioritize ethical implementation**: Ensure the responsible and transparent use of generative AI, emphasizing ethical practices to build trust and minimize unintended consequences.
- **Invest in innovation**: Explore the full potential of generative AI applications and allocate resources to their development to drive innovative solutions and competitive advantages.
- **Foster talent development**: Cultivate a skilled workforce adept at harnessing generative AI, emphasizing

continuous learning and upskilling to maximize its potential.

- **Take it slow and control your circus and your AI musicians**: Approach the adoption of generative AI with caution and control. Rushing into implementation without careful consideration of its implications can lead to unintended chaos and risks. Manage the process deliberately, ensuring controlled and measured adoption to maximize benefits and minimize disruptions.

- **Maintain agility and adaptability**: Stay flexible and responsive to changes in the landscape, proactively integrating generative AI into strategic planning for sustained relevance and growth.

- **Settle in for the long haul**: Understand that AI, like data, is an ongoing journey. Technology landscapes evolve, and the battle for big tech market relevance has only just begun. Laws and regulations surrounding AI will continue to evolve, making a long-term commitment to AI evolution crucial for sustained success.

Generative AI's trajectory will significantly influence the future of data and analytics, reshaping organizational approaches to data utilization and decision-making. Executives who embrace this ongoing journey and adapt to evolving landscapes, including regulatory changes, will lead their organizations to innovative, ethical, and impactful data-driven strategies, ensuring future success and relevance.

Conclusion: Embracing the future of data and AI

In the culmination of this transformative journey through the realms of AI evolution, the rise of generative AI, and the required spotlight on data, organizations stand at the precipice of a groundbreaking era—a juncture where innovation intertwines with necessity, and foresight meets execution. The voyage through *Unleashing the Power of Data with Trusted AI* has been an expedition into the heart of data and technological evolution, guided by expertise and foresight into the AI, data, and software fields.

- **Charting a new frontier**: The roadmap unveiled within these pages was designed to steer executives, board members, and visionaries into uncharted territories where data reigns as the irrefutable currency of progress. The insights, experiences, and strategies unveiled herein serve as beacons illuminating the path toward a future sculpted by informed decisions, innovation, and strategic mastery.

- **Beyond insight to action**: However, true transformation lies not in mere insights but in the application of knowledge. As we navigate the constantly evolving landscapes of data and AI, the definitive understanding derived from this guide acts as a catalyst, propelling organizations toward meaningful action, innovative leaps, and evolutionary shifts.

- **Ethical imperative and responsible innovation**: The ethical compass guiding every facet of AI implementation cannot be understated. As we venture forth into the boundless frontier of technology, the governance, responsibility, and ethical considerations embedded within the strategies delineated here are the moral guardians, ensuring that progress is not only transformative but also ethical, responsible, and trust-inducing.

- **Data by Design – a new paradigm**: The revelation of Data by Design stands as the cornerstone—a paradigm shift in the very fabric of data strategy. Its integration into organizational DNA acts as an assurance of resilience, aligning strategic imperatives with data practices, and fortifying the foundation upon which innovation thrives.

- **The future beckons**: As we bid adieu to you in the final pages of this guide, the journey does not conclude here. Instead, it becomes the launchpad for a future where data is not just a resource but the fulcrum upon which entire industries pivot, where AI is not a tool but a harbinger of transformation.

- **Charting course for data-driven excellence**: The future is ripe with possibilities, brimming with innovations yet to be discovered. It's an era where executives and leaders, armed with the wisdom from these chapters, will orchestrate strategies that revolutionize industries, redefine paradigms, and set sail toward a horizon where data-driven excellence reigns supreme.

- **Armed with insight, ignite the future**: Let the insights gleaned from these pages be the catalyst, the inspiration that fuels the flames of innovation. May these revelations spur progressive thinking, informed decision-making, and the audacity to embrace change fearlessly.

As we close this report, it's not an end but a prelude—a prelude to the unending saga of innovation, transformation, and pioneering strides in the ever-evolving landscape of data and AI.

About the author

Wendy Turner-Williams is:

- Founder and CEO of *TheAssociation.ai and Culstrata-ai*
- Adjunct Professor at *Carnegie Mellon University Heinz College C-DATA-O*
- Adjunct Professor at *MIT CDO IQ Institute*
- Advisory Board Member at *University of Washington Informatics School*
- Former Chief Data and AI Officer at *Tableau and Salesforce*

Wendy is a distinguished leader and innovator at the intersection of business, AI, data, and software. With over two decades of experience, she has been instrumental in spearheading digital, cloud, and AI transformations across globally recognized brands, translating complex concepts into actionable strategies that drive significant growth, efficiency, and customer trust. Her expertise is not just in leading and executing data or technological advancements but also in fostering culture change, promoting cross-functional collaboration, and advocating and designing successful human-centric designed solutions and self-service architectures.

As the founder and CEO of *Culstrata-ai* and *TheAssociation.ai*, Wendy has created platforms that not only provide professional AI and data services but also globally unite professionals across the fields of AI, data, ethics, privacy, robotics, and security in promoting an ethical, quality, and trustworthy AI future. Her leadership role as chief data and AI officer at Salesforce, Tableau, and other tech giants reflects her ability to realize substantial revenue and operational advancements. Her unique experience as an architect, data professional, and big tech technologist has led to the creation of numerous products and services, and a direct impact of $1.4 billion ARR.

Wendy is a prolific author, speaker, and thought leader, sharing her insights on AI, the cloud, data, and leadership. Her commitment extends beyond professional realms as she actively contributes to Women in Technology and Women in Data communities, advocating for diversity, equity, inclusion, chronic illness awareness, and blood/plasma donations. Wendy's academic background in History from Oklahoma State University adds a unique perspective to her technological and leadership prowess.

As a mother of four girls, Wendy embodies the balance between personal commitment and professional excellence, making her a role model and an inspiration for aspiring leaders in technology and beyond. Her comprehensive approach and dedication to ethical practices in AI and data make her a luminary in her field, driving positive change and innovation for all.

Bibliography

1. PricewaterhouseCoopers. n.d. "PWC's Global Artificial Intelligence Study: Sizing the Prize." PwC. Accessed February 9, 2024. https://www.pwc.com/gx/en/issues/data-and-analytics/publications/artificial-intelligence-study.html.

2. Panel®, Expert. 2023. "Council Post: 19 Ways AI May Soon Revolutionize the Healthcare Industry." Forbes. Forbes Magazine. October 5, 2023. https://www.forbes.com/sites/forbestechcouncil/2023/04/18/19-ways-ai-may-soon-revolutionize-the-healthcare-industry/?sh=59b4a6dd1bb8.

3. Italie, Hillel. 2023. "'Game of Thrones' Creator and Other Authors Sue Chatgpt-Maker Openai for Copyright Infringement." AP News. AP News. September 21, 2023. https://apnews.com/article/openai-lawsuit-authors-grisham-george-rr-martin-37f9073ab67ab25b7e6b2975b2a63bfe.

4. N.d. New York Regulator Probes UnitedHealth Algorithm for Racial Bias - WSJ. Accessed February 9, 2024. https://www.wsj.com/articles/new-york-regulator-probes-unitedhealth-algorithm-for-racial-bias-11572087601.

5. Ferguson, H. (2024, May 22). New Research: What Boardroom Leaders Think About Generative AI. Alteryx. https://www.alteryx.com/blog/what-boardroom-leaders-think-about-generative-ai.

6. Business Wire. (2022, January 3). https://www.businesswire.com/news/home/20220103005036/en/NewVantage-Partners-Releases-2022-Data-And-AI-Executive-Survey.

7. Drenik, Gary. 2023. "Data Quality For Good AI Outcomes." Forbes. https://www.forbes.com/sites/garydrenik/2023/08/15/data-quality-for-good-ai-outcomes/?sh=53f923ea1184.

8. Chui, Michael, and Bryce Hall. 2020. "How High Performing Companies Develop and Scale AI." McKinsey & Company. McKinsey & Company. March 23, 2020. https://www.mckinsey.com/mgi/overview/in-the-news/how-high-performing-companies-develop-and-scale-ai.

9. Turner-Williams, Wendy. n.d. "5 Ways CDOs Must Act as Data Conductors." Data Leadership Collaborative. Accessed February 9, 2024. https://www.dataleadershipcollaborative.com/data-leadership/5-ways-cdos-must-act-data-conductors.

10. Artificial Intelligence Accountability Policy | National Telecommunications and Information Administration. (n.d.). https://www.ntia.gov/issues/artificial-intelligence/ai-accountability-policy-report/overvie.

11. Adita Karkera, Mike Greene, Landon Henderson, & Jonathan Newman. (n.d.). Is your data AI-ready? Deloitte. https://www2.deloitte.com/content/dam/Deloitte/us/Documents/public-sector/is-your-data-ai-ready.pdf.

12. "Cloud Data - CDMC." Cloud Data - CDMC - EDM Council. Accessed February 9, 2024. https://edmcouncil.org/frameworks/cdmc/.

13. DAMA, January 5, 2024. https://www.dama.org/cpages/home.

14. Pushkarna, Mahima, Andrew Zaldivar, and Oddur Kjartansson. "Data Cards: Purposeful and Transparent Dataset Documentation for Responsible Ai." arxiv.org, April 3, 2022. https://arxiv.org/abs/2204.01075.

15. Bansal, Manu. 2022. "Council Post: Flying Blind: How Bad Data Undermines Business." Forbes. Forbes Magazine. November 9, 2022. https://www.forbes.com/sites/forbestechcouncil/2021/10/14/flying-blind-how-bad-data-undermines-business/?sh=277afbdf29e8.

16. "Executive Order on the Safe, Secure, and Trustworthy Development and Use of Artificial Intelligence." The White House, October 30, 2023. https://www.whitehouse.gov/briefing-room/presidential-actions/2023/10/30/executive-order-on-the-safe-secure-and-trustworthy-development-and-use-of-artificial-intelligence/.

17. "A European Approach to Artificial Intelligence." Shaping Europe's digital future. Accessed February 9, 2024. https://digital-strategy.ec.europa.eu/en/policies/european-approach-artificial-intelligence.

18. Michael. "The Times Sues OpenAI and Microsoft over A.I. Use of Copyrighted Work." The New York Times, December 27, 2023. https://www.nytimes.com/2023/12/27/business/media/new-york-times-open-ai-microsoft-lawsuit.html.

19. "Generative AI Has an Intellectual Property Problem." Harvard Business Review, April 11, 2023. https://hbr.org/2023/04/generative-ai-has-an-intellectual-property-problem.

20. "Ethics of Artificial Intelligence." UNESCO.org. Accessed February 9, 2024. https://www.unesco.org/en/artificial-intelligence/recommendation-ethics.

21. Truly, Alan, and Jacob Roach. "Zoom Backpedals on Training Its AI Models." Digital Trends, August 11, 2023. https://www.digitaltrends.com/computing/zoom-can-train-ai-on-your-videos-what-you-need-to-know/.

22. Henriquez, Maria. "The Top 10 Data Breaches of 2020." Security Magazine RSS, December 8, 2021. https://www.securitymagazine.com/articles/94076-the-top-10-data-breaches-of-2020.

23. "Cybersecurity Framework." NIST, February 1, 2024. https://www.nist.gov/cyberframework.

24. Team, Insights. "Forbes Insights: Behind Every AI Strategy Is a Data Strategy." Forbes, December 14, 2018. https://www.forbes.com/sites/insights-delltechnologies/2018/12/04/behind-every-ai-strategy-is-a-data-strategy/?sh=37ce75bf1d4c.

25. Newberry, Christina. "74 Artificial Intelligence Statistics to Guide Your Marketing Plan." Social Media Marketing & Management Dashboard, August 17, 2023. https://blog.hootsuite.com/artificial-intelligence-statistics/.

26. "Official Legal Text." General Data Protection Regulation (GDPR), September 27, 2022. https://gdpr-info.eu/.

27. "California Consumer Privacy Act (CCPA)." State of California - Department of Justice - Office of the Attorney General, November 9, 2023. https://oag.ca.gov/privacy/ccpa.

28. McCallum, Shiona. "Meta: Facebook Owner Fined €1.2bn for Mishandling Data." BBC News, May 22, 2023. https://www.bbc.com/news/technology-65669839.

29. France fines Google $57 million for European privacy rule breach. Accessed February 9, 2024. https://www.reuters.com/article/idUSKCN1PF1ZH.

30. Solomons, M. (2024, February 23). 90 AI Statistics: Applications, Design Principles, and Challenges. Linearity Blog. https://tinyurl.com/3y32hujm.

31. Maheshwari, R. (2024, February 6). Top AI Statistics And Trends. Forbes Advisor INDIA. https://www.forbes.com/advisor/in/business/ai-statistics/.

32. Maheshwari, R. (2024b, February 6). Top AI Statistics And Trends. Forbes Advisor INDIA. https://www.forbes.com/advisor/in/business/ai-statistics/.

33. Maheshwari, R. (2024c, February 6). Top AI Statistics And Trends. Forbes Advisor INDIA. https://www.forbes.com/advisor/in/business/ai-statistics/.

34. Soper, Taylor. "How Digital Initiatives and Artificial Intelligence Continue Fueling Innovation at Starbucks." GeekWire, November 1, 2019. https://www.geekwire.com/2019/digital-initiatives-artificial-intelligence-continue-fueling-innovation-starbucks/.

35. Pymnts. (2024, January 31). Starbucks Uses AI-Powered Personalized Rewards to Boost Frequency and Spend. PYMNTS.com. https://www.pymnts.com/news/loyalty-and-rewards-news/2024/starbucks-uses-artificial-intelligence-powered-personalized-rewards-boost-frequency-check-size/.

36. "Informit." InformIT. Accessed February 9, 2024. https://www.informit.com/articles/article.aspx?p=2992600&seqNum=6#:~:text=Costing%20%24250%20million%20to%20build,tons%20of%20greenhouse%20gas%20emissions.

37. Leonard, M. (2021, June 11). UPS adds dynamic routing to ORION, saving 2-4 miles per driver. Supply Chain Dive. https://www.supplychaindive.com/news/ups-orion-route-planning-analytics-data-logistics/601673/.

38. "Netflix Techblog." Netflix TechBlog. Accessed February 9, 2024. https://netflixtechblog.com/.

39. Plummer, L. (2017, August 22). This is how Netflix's top-secret recommendation system works. WIRED. https://www.wired.com/story/how-do-netflixs-algorithms-work-machine-learning-helps-to-predict-what-viewers-will-like/.

40. Siemens Manufacturing. (n.d.). https://siemensmfg.com/.

41. The Future of Generative AI. (2024, March 7). AI, Data & Analytics Network. https://www.aidataanalytics.network/datascience-ai/articles/the-future-of-generative-ai.

Other books you may enjoy

If you enjoyed this book, you may be interested in these other books by Packt:

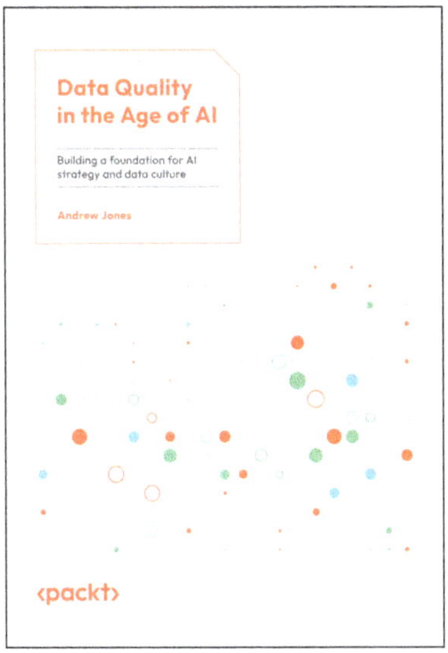

Data Quality in the Age of AI

Andrew Jones

ISBN: 978-1-80512-143-5

- Elevate data quality and enhance data literacy within your organization
- Craft effective AI strategies for data analytics processes
- Explore real-world case studies showcasing the tangible benefits of trusted AI
- Optimize decision-making processes by harnessing AI-driven insights
- Gain comprehensive insights and analyses to make quick and accurate decisions
- Learn to integrate trusted AI into your organizational workflows and decision-making processes

Packt is searching for authors like you

If you're interested in becoming an author for Packt, please visit authors.packtpub.com and apply today. We have worked with thousands of developers and tech professionals, just like you, to help them share their insight with the global tech community. You can make a general application, apply for a specific hot topic that we are recruiting an author for, or submit your own idea.

www.ingramcontent.com/pod-product-compliance
Lightning Source LLC
LaVergne TN
LVHW060043210926
848481LV00013B/3942
* 9 7 8 1 8 3 5 4 6 7 8 9 3 *